LAMENT FOR THE MAKERS

POETRY BY W. S. MERWIN

The Vixen   1996

Travels   1993

The Second Four Books of Poems   1993
(including the complete texts of *The Moving Target, The Lice,
The Carrier of Ladders,* and *Writings to an Unfinished Accompaniment*)

Selected Poems   1988

The Rain in the Trees   1988

Opening the Hand   1983

Finding the Islands   1982

The Compass Flower   1977

The First Four Books of Poems   1975
(including the complete texts of *A Mask for Janus, The Dancing Bears,
Green with Beasts,* and *The Drunk in the Furnace*)

Writings to an Unfinished Accompaniment   1973

The Carrier of Ladders   1970

The Lice   1967

The Moving Target   1963

The Drunk in the Furnace   1960

Green with Beasts   1956

The Dancing Bears   1954

A Mask for Janus   1952

LAMENT FOR THE MAKERS

A MEMORIAL ANTHOLOGY

W. S. MERWIN

COUNTERPOINT

BERKELEY

LIBRARY OF CONGRESS CATALOGING-IN-PUBLICATION DATA
Lament for the makers: a memorial anthology /
[compiled by] W.S. Merwin

1. American poetry—20th century. 2. English poetry—20th century.
1. Merwin, W.S. (William Stanley), 1927–
PS613.L36   1996
811'. 508—dc20   96-26706

ISBN 978-1-58243-732-3

Design and electronic production by David Bullen

COUNTERPOINT
1919 Fifth Street
Berkeley, CA 94710

www.counterpointpress.com

Distributed by Publishers Group West

10 9 8 7 6 5 4 3 2 1

CONTENTS

LAMENT FOR THE MAKERS

A MEMORIAL ANTHOLOGY

W. S. MERWIN

LAMENT FOR THE MAKERS

I that all through my early days
I remember well was always
    the youngest of the company
    save for one sister after me

from the time when I was able
to walk under the dinner table
    and be punished for that promptly
    because its leaves could fall on me

father and mother overhead
who they talked with and what they said
    were mostly clouds that knew already
    directions far too old for me

at school I skipped a grade so that
whatever I did after that
    each year everyone would be
    older and hold it up to me

at college many of my friends
were returning veterans
      equipped with an authority
      I admired and they treated me

as the kid some years below them
so I married half to show them
      and listened with new vanity
      when I heard it said of me

how young I was and what a shock
I was the youngest on the block
      I thought I had it coming to me
      and I believe it mattered to me

and seemed my own and there to stay
for a while then came the day
      I was in another country
      other older friends around me

my youth by then taken for granted
and found that it had been supplanted
      the notes in some anthology
      listed persons born after me

how long had that been going on
how could I be not quite so young
        and not notice and nobody
        even bother to inform me

though my fond hopes were taking longer
than I had hoped when I was younger
        a phrase that came more frequently
        to suggest itself to me

but the secret was still there
safe in the unprotected air
        that breath that in its own words only
        sang when I was a child to me

and caught me helpless to convey it
with nothing but the words to say it
        though it was those words completely
        and they rang it was clear to me

with a changeless overtone
I have listened for since then
        hearing that note endlessly
        vary every time beyond me

trying to find where it comes from
and to what words it may come
  and forever after be
  present for the thought kept at me

that my mother and every day
of our lives would slip away
  like the summer and suddenly
  all would have been taken from me

but that presence I had known
sometimes in words would not be gone
  and if it spoke even once for me
  it would stay there and be me

however few might choose those words
for listening to afterwards
  there I would be awake to see
  a world that looked unchanged to me

I suppose that was what I thought
young as I was then and that note
  sang from the words of somebody
  in my twenties I looked around me

to all the poets who were then
living and whose lines had been
      sustenance and company
      and a light for years to me

I found the portraits of their faces
first in the rows of oval spaces
      in Oscar Williams' *Treasury*
      so they were settled long before me

and they would always be the same
in that distance of their fame
      affixed in immortality
      during their lifetimes while around me

all was woods seen from a train
no sooner glimpsed than gone again
      but those immortals constantly
      in some measure reassured me

then first there was Dylan Thomas
from the White Horse taken from us
      to the brick wall I woke to see
      for years across the street from me

then word of the death of Stevens
brought a new knowledge of silence
        the nothing not there finally
        the sparrow saying *Bethou me*

how long his long auroras had
played on the darkness overhead
        since I looked up from my Shelley
        and Arrowsmith first showed him to me

and not long from his death until
Edwin Muir had fallen still
        that fine bell of the latter day
        not well heard yet it seems to me

Sylvia Plath then took her own
direction into the unknown
        from her last stars and poetry
        in the house a few blocks from me

Williams a little afterwards
was carried off by the black rapids
        that flowed through Paterson as he
        said and their rushing sound is in me

that was the time that gathered Frost
into the dark where he was lost
      to us but from too far to see
      his voice keeps coming back to me

then the sudden news that Ted
Roethke had been found floating dead
      in someone's pool at night but he
      still rises from his lines for me

MacNeice watched the cold light harden
when that day had left the garden
      stepped into the dark ground to see
      where it went but never told me

and on the rimless wheel in turn
Eliot spun and Jarrell was borne
      off by a car who had loved to see
      the racetrack then there came to me

one day the knocking at the garden
door and the news that Berryman
      from the bridge had leapt who twenty
      years before had quoted to me

the passage where *a jest* wrote Crane
falls from the speechless caravan
        with a wave to bones and Henry
        and to all that he had told me

I dreamed that Auden sat up in bed
but I could not catch what he said
        by that time he was already
        dead someone next morning told me

and Marianne Moore entered the ark
Pound would say no more from the dark
        who once had helped to set me free
        I thought of the prose around me

and David Jones would rest until
the turn of time under the hill
        but from the sleep of Arthur he
        wakes an echo that follows me

Lowell thought the shadow skyline
coming toward him was Manhattan
        but it blacked out in the taxi
        once he read his *Notebook* to me

at the number he had uttered
to the driver a last word
     then that watchful and most lonely
     wanderer whose words went with me

everywhere Elizabeth
Bishop lay alone in death
     they were leaving the party early
     our elders it came home to me

but the needle moved among us
taking always by surprise
     flicking by too fast to see
     to touch a friend born after me

and James Wright by his darkened river
heard the night heron pass over
     took his candle down the frosty
     road and disappeared before me

Howard Moss had felt the gnawing
at his name and found that nothing
     made it better he was funny
     even so about it to me

Graves in his nineties lost the score
forgot that he had died before
        found his way back innocently
        who once had been a guide to me

Nemerov sadder than his verse
said a new year could not be worse
        then the black flukes of agony
        went down leaving the words with me

Stafford watched his hand catch the light
seeing that it was time to write
        a memento of their story
        signed and is a plain before me

now Jimmy Merrill's voice is heard
like an aria afterward
        and we know he will never be
        old after all who spoke to me

on the cold street that last evening
of his heart that leapt at finding
        some yet unknown poetry
        then waved through the window to me

in that city we were born in
one by one they have all gone
       out of the time and language we
       had in common which have brought me

to this season after them
the best words did not keep them from
       leaving themselves finally
       as this day is going from me

and the clear note they were hearing
never promised anything
       but the true sound of brevity
       that will go on after me

DYLAN THOMAS

A REFUSAL TO MOURN THE DEATH, BY FIRE, OF A CHILD IN LONDON

Never until the mankind making
Bird beast and flower
Fathering and all humbling darkness
Tells with silence the last light breaking
And the still hour
Is come of the sea tumbling in harness

And I must enter again the round
Zion of the water bead
And the synagogue of the ear of corn
Shall I let pray the shadow of a sound
Or sow my salt seed
In the least valley of sackcloth to mourn

The majesty and burning of the child's death.
I shall not murder
The mankind of her going with a grave truth
Nor blaspheme down the stations of the breath
With any further
Elegy of innocence and youth.

Deep with the first dead lies London's daughter,
Robed in the long friends,
The grains beyond age, the dark veins of her mother,
Secret by the unmourning water
Of the riding Thames.
After the first death, there is no other.

Dylan Thomas was born on October 27, 1914, in Swansea, Wales. He spent his childhood holidays on his grandparents' farm in southwestern Wales; many of his poems, including those collected in his fourth volume, Deaths and Entrances *(1946), are complexly wrought explorations of the joys of that youth. Thomas also wrote stories and plays. His "play for voices,"* Under Milkwood, *was published in 1954. He died in New York City on November 9, 1953.*

WALLACE STEVENS

THE RIVER OF RIVERS IN CONNECTICUT

There is a great river this side of Stygia,
Before one comes to the first black cataracts
And trees that lack the intelligence of trees.

In that river, far this side of Stygia,
The mere flowing of the water is a gayety,
Flashing and flashing in the sun. On its banks,

No shadow walks. The river is fateful,
Like the last one. But there is no ferryman.
He could not bend against its propelling force.

It is not to be seen beneath the appearances
That tell of it. The steeple at Farmington
Stands glistening and Haddam shines and sways.

It is the third commonness with light and air,
A curriculum, a vigor, a local abstraction . . .
Call it, once more, a river, an unnamed flowing,

Space-filled, reflecting the seasons, the folk-lore
Of each of the senses; call it, again and again,
The river that flows nowhere, like a sea.

Wallace Stevens was born on October 2, 1879, in Reading, Pennsylvania. A lawyer by training, Stevens worked for the Hartford Accident and Indemnity Company, and became its vice-president in 1934. His books include Harmonium, The Man with the Blue Guitar, The Auroras of Autumn, *and the* Collected Poems, *for which he received the Pulitzer Prize in 1954. Stevens died on August 2, 1955, in Hartford, Connecticut.*

EDWIN MUIR

THE ANIMALS

They do not live in the world,
Are not in time and space.
From birth to death hurled
No word do they have, not one
To plant a foot upon,
Were never in any place.

For with names the world was called
Out of the empty air,
With names was built and walled,
Line and circle and square,
Dust and emerald;

Snatched from deceiving death
By the articulate breath.
But these have never trod
Twice the familiar track,
Never never turned back
Into the memoried day.

All is new and near
In the unchanging Here
Of the fifth great day of God,
That shall remain the same,
Never shall pass away.

On the sixth day we came.

Edwin Muir was born on May 15, 1887, in Deerness, Scotland. His reputation as one of the foremost Scottish poets of his day was firmly established after the publication of The Voyage *(1946) and* The Labyrinth *(1949). Muir and his wife, Willa Anderson, were also distinguished by their translations of Hermann Broch's* Sleepwalkers *and of Franz Kafka's work. Muir died on January 3, 1959, in Cambridge, England.*

SYLVIA PLATH

WORDS

Axes
After whose stroke the wood rings,
And the echoes!
Echoes travelling
Off from the centre like horses.

The sap
Wells like tears, like the
Water striving
To re-establish its mirror
Over the rock

That drops and turns,
A white skull,
Eaten by weedy greens.
Years later I
Encounter them on the road—

Words dry and riderless,
The indefatigable hoof-taps.
While
From the bottom of the pool, fixed stars
Govern a life.

Sylvia Plath was born on October 27, 1932, in Boston. Although Plath's The Colossus *(1960) was her first major pub-lication, she was little known until* Ariel *was published posthumously in 1965. Plath was also the author of the novel* The Bell Jar *(1963). She committed suicide in London on February 11, 1963.*

WILLIAM CARLOS WILLIAMS

SPRING AND ALL

By the road to the contagious hospital
under the surge of the blue
mottled clouds driven from the
northeast—a cold wind. Beyond, the
waste of broad, muddy fields
brown with dried weeds, standing and fallen

patches of standing water
the scattering of tall trees

All along the road the reddish
purplish, forked, upstanding, twiggy
stuff of bushes and small trees
with dead, brown leaves under them
leafless vines—

Lifeless in appearance, sluggish
dazed spring approaches—

They enter the new world naked,
cold, uncertain of all
save that they enter. All about them
the cold, familiar wind—

Now the grass, tomorrow
the stiff curl of wildcarrot leaf
One by one objects are defined—
It quickens: clarity, outline of leaf

But now the stark dignity of
entrance—Still, the profound change
has come upon them: rooted, they
grip down and begin to awaken

William Carlos Williams was born on September 17, 1883, in Rutherford, New Jersey. A doctor in practice, Williams wrote many influential books of poetry, including Paterson, *which was published in five volumes from 1946 to 1958. He was awarded the Pulitzer Prize posthumously in 1963 for* Pictures from Brueghel. *His books of prose include the study* In the American Grain *(1925). He died on March 4, 1963, in Rutherford.*

ROBERT FROST

NEITHER OUT FAR NOR IN DEEP

The people along the sand
All turn and look one way.
They turn their back on the land.
They look at the sea all day.

As long as it takes to pass
A ship keeps raising its hull;
The wetter ground like glass
Reflects a standing gull.

The land may vary more;
But wherever the truth may be—
The water comes ashore,
And the people look at the sea.

They cannot look out far.
They cannot look in deep.
But when was that ever a bar
To any watch they keep?

Robert Frost was born on March 26, 1874, in San Francisco. When he was eleven, his widowed mother moved the family to Massachusetts. Frost's first two books, A Boy's Will *(1913) and* North of Boston *(1914) were published in England before his poetry was noticed in America. Frost was awarded the Pulitzer Prize four times. He died on January 29, 1963, in Boston.*

THEODORE ROETHKE

MEDITATIONS OF AN OLD WOMAN

First Meditation

I

On love's worst ugly day,
The weeds hiss at the edge of the field,
The small winds make their chilly indictments.
Elsewhere, in houses, even pails can be sad;

While stones loosen on the obscure hillside,
And a tree tilts from its roots,
Toppling down an embankment.

The spirit moves, but not always upward,
While animals eat to the north,
And the shale slides an inch in the talus,
The bleak wind eats at the weak plateau,
And the sun brings joy to some.
But the rind, often, hates the life within.

How can I rest in the days of my slowness?
I've become a strange piece of flesh,
Nervous and cold, bird-furtive, whiskery,
With a cheek soft as a hound's ear.
What's left is light as a seed;
I need an old crone's knowing.

2

Often I think of myself as riding—
Alone, on a bus through western country.
I sit above the back wheels, where the jolts are hardest,
And we bounce and sway along toward the midnight,
The lights tilting up, skyward, as we come over a little rise,
Then down, as we roll like a boat from a wave-crest.

All journeys, I think, are the same:
The movement is forward, after a few wavers,
And for a while we are all alone,
Busy, obvious with ourselves,
The drunken soldier, the old lady with her peppermints;
And we ride, we ride, taking the curves
Somewhat closer, the trucks coming
Down from behind the last ranges,
Their black shapes breaking past;
And the air claps between us,
Blasting the frosted windows,
And I seem to go backward,
Backward in time:

        Two song sparrows, one within a greenhouse,
        Shuttling its throat while perched on a wind-vent,
        And another, outside, in the bright day,
        With a wind from the west and trees all in motion.
        One sang, then the other,
        The songs tumbling over and under the glass,
        And the men beneath them wheeling in dirt to the cement benches,
        The laden wheelbarrows creaking and swaying,
        And the up-spring of the plank when a foot left the runway.

Journey within a journey:
The ticket mislaid or lost, the gate
Inaccessible, the boat always pulling out
From the rickety wooden dock,
The children waving;
Or two horses plunging in snow, their lines tangled,
A great wooden sleigh careening behind them,
Swerving up a steep embankment.
For a moment they stand above me,
Their black skins shuddering:
Then they lurch forward,
Lunging down a hillside.

3

As when silt drifts and sifts down through muddy pond-water,
Settling in small beads around weeds and sunken branches,
And one crab, tentative, hunches himself before moving along the bottom,
Grotesque, awkward, his extended eyes looking at nothing in particular,
Only a few bubbles loosening from the ill-matched tentacles,
The tail and smaller legs slipping and sliding slowly backward—
So the spirit tries for another life,
Another way and place in which to continue;
Or a salmon, tired, moving up a shallow stream,

Nudges into a back-eddy, a sandy inlet,
Bumping against sticks and bottom-stones, then swinging
Around, back into the tiny maincurrent, the rush of brownish-white water,
Still swimming forward—
So, I suppose, the spirit journeys.

4

I have gone into the waste lonely places
Behind the eye; the lost acres at the edge of smoky cities.
What's beyond never crumbles like an embankment,
Explodes like a rose, or thrusts wings over the Caribbean.
There are no pursuing forms, faces on walls:
Only the motes of dust in the immaculate hallways,
The darkness of falling hair, the warnings from lint and spiders,
The vines graying to a fine powder.
There is no riven tree, or lamb dropped by an eagle.

There are still times, morning and evening:
The cerulean, high in the elm,
Thin and insistent as a cicada,
And the far phoebe, singing,
The long plaintive notes floating down,
Drifting through leaves, oak and maple,

Or the whippoorwill, along the smoky ridges,
A single bird calling and calling;
A fume reminds me, drifting across wet gravel;
A cold wind comes over stones;
A flame, intense, visible,
Plays over the dry pods,
Runs fitfully along the stubble,
Moves over the field,
Without burning.
      In such times, lacking a god,
      I am still happy.

Theodore Roethke was born on May 25, 1908, in Saginaw, Michigan. He taught for fifteen years at the University of Washington and was made poet in residence there in 1962. The Waking: Poems 1933–1953 *won the Pulitzer Prize in 1954. He was awarded the Bollingen Prize and the National Book Award in 1958 for* Words for the Wind: The Collected Poems. *He died on August 1, 1963, in Seattle.*

LOUIS MACNEICE

AUTUMN JOURNAL VII

Conferences, adjournments, ultimatums,
  Flights in the air, castles in the air,
The autopsy of treaties, dynamite under the bridges,
  The end of *laissez faire.*
After the warm days the rain comes pimpling
  The paving stones with white
And with the rain the national conscience, creeping,
  Seeping through the night.

And in the sodden park on Sunday protest
  Meetings assemble not, as so often, now
Merely to advertise some patent panacea
  But simply to avow
The need to hold the ditch; a bare avowal
  That may perhaps imply
Death at the doors in a week but perhaps in the long run
  Exposure of the lie.
Think of a number, double it, treble it, square it,
  And sponge it out
And repeat *ad lib.* and mark the slate with crosses;
  There is no time to doubt
If the puzzle really has an answer. Hitler yells on the wireless,
  The night is damp and still
And I hear dull blows on wood outside my window;
  They are cutting down the trees on Primrose Hill.
The wood is white like the roast flesh of chicken,
  Each tree falling like a closing fan;
No more looking at the view from seats beneath the branches,
  Everything is going to plan;
They want the crest of this hill for anti-aircraft,
  The guns will take the view
And searchlights probe the heavens for bacilli
  With narrow wands of blue.
And the rain came on as I watched the territorials
  Sawing and chopping and pulling on ropes like a team

In a village tug-of-war; and I found my dog had vanished
  And thought 'This is the end of the old régime,'
But found the police had got her at St. John's Wood station
  And fetched her in the rain and went for a cup
Of coffee to an all-night shelter and heard a taxi-driver
  Say 'It turns me up

When I see these soldiers in lorries'—rumble of tumbrils
  Drums in the trees
Breaking the eardrums of the ravished dryads—
  It turns me up; a coffee, please.
And as I go out I see a windscreen-wiper
  In an empty car
Wiping away like mad and I feel astounded
  That things have gone so far.
And I come back here to my flat and wonder whether
  From now on I need take
The trouble to go out choosing stuff for curtains
  As I don't know anyone to make
Curtains quickly. Rather one should quickly
  stop the cracks for gas or dig a trench
And take one's paltry measures against the coming
  Of the unknown Uebermensch.
But one—meaning I—is bored, am bored, the issue
  Involving principle but bound in fact
To squander principle in panic and self-deception—
  Accessories after the act,

So that all we foresee is rivers in spate sprouting
  With drowning hands
And men like dead frogs floating till the rivers
  Lose themselves in the sands.
And we who have been brought up to think of 'Gallant Belgium'
  As so much blague
Are now preparing again to essay good through evil
  For the sake of Prague;
And must, we suppose, become uncritical, vindictive,
  And must, in order to beat
The enemy, model ourselves upon the enemy,
  A howling radio for our paraclete.
The night continues wet, the axe keeps falling,
  The hill grows bald and bleak
No longer one of the sights of London but maybe
  We shall have fireworks here by this day week.

Louis MacNeice was born on September 12, 1907, in Belfast. Together with W. H. Auden, Stephen Spender, and others, MacNeice practiced the "new poetry" of the 1930s, which, among other things, was plain, socially committed, and topical. His books include Blind Fireworks *and* Autumn Journal. *He died on September 3, 1963, in London.*

T. S. ELIOT

LITTLE GIDDING
from Four Quartets

I

Midwinter spring is its own season
Sempiternal though sodden towards sundown,
Suspended in time, between pole and tropic.
When the short day is brightest, with frost and fire,

The brief sun flames the ice, on pond and ditches,
In windless cold that is the heart's heat,
Reflecting in a watery mirror
A glare that is blindness in the early afternoon.
And glow more intense than blaze of branch, or brazier,
Stirs the dumb spirit: no wind, but pentecostal fire
In the dark time of the year. Between melting and freezing
The soul's sap quivers. There is no earth smell
Or smell of living thing. This is the spring time
But not in time's covenant. Now the hedgerow
Is blanched for an hour with transitory blossom
Of snow, a bloom more sudden
Than that of summer, neither budding nor fading,
Not in the scheme of generation.
Where is the summer, the unimaginable
Zero summer?

   If you came this way,
Taking the route you would be likely to take
From the place you would be likely to come from,
If you came this way in may time, you would find the hedges
White again, in May, with voluptuary sweetness.
It would be the same at the end of the journey,
If you came at night like a broken king,
If you came by day not knowing what you came for,

It would be the same, when you leave the rough road
And turn behind the pig-sty to the dull façade
And the tombstone. And what you thought you came for
Is only a shell, a husk of meaning
From which the purpose breaks only when it is fulfilled
If at all. Either you had no purpose
Or the purpose is beyond the end you figured
And is altered in fulfillment. There are other places
Which also are the world's end, some at the sea jaws,
Or over a dark lake, in a desert or a city—
But this is the nearest, in place and time,
Now and in England.

          If you came this way,
Taking any route, starting from anywhere,
At any time or at any season,
It would always be the same: you would have to put off
Sense and notion. You are not here to verify,
Instruct yourself, or inform curiosity
Or carry report. You are here to kneel
Where prayer has been valid. And prayer is more
Than an order of words, the conscious occupation
Of the praying mind, or the sound of the voice praying.
And what the dead had no speech for, when living,

They can tell you, being dead: the communication
Of the dead is tongued with fire beyond the language of the living.
Here, the intersection of the timeless moment
Is England and nowhere. Never and always.

II

Ash on an old man's sleeve
Is all the ash the burnt roses leave.
Dust in the air suspended
Marks the place where a story ended.
Dust inbreathed was a house—
The wall, the wainscot and the mouse.
The death of hope and despair,
      This is the death of air.

   There are flood and drouth
Over the eyes and in the mouth,
Dead water and dead sand
Contending for the upper hand.
The parched eviscerate soil
Gapes at the vanity of the toil,
Laughs without mirth.
      This is the death of earth.

Water and fire succeed
The town, the pasture and the weed.
Water and fire deride
The sacrifice that we denied.
Water and fire shall rot
The marred foundations we forgot,
Of sanctuary and choir.
This is the death of water and fire.

In the uncertain hour before the morning
Near the ending of interminable night
At the recurrent end of the unending
After the dark dove with the flickering tongue
Had passed below the horizon of his homing
While the dead leaves still rattled on like tin
Over the asphalt where no other sound was
Between three districts whence the smoke arose
I met one walking, loitering and hurried
As if blown towards me like the metal leaves
Before the urban dawn wind unresisting.
And as I fixed upon the down-turned face
That pointed scrutiny with which we challenge
The first-met stranger in the waning dusk
I caught the sudden look of some dead master

Whom I had known, forgotten, half recalled
   Both one and many; in the brown baked features
   The eyes of a familiar compound ghost
Both intimate and unidentifiable.
   So I assumed a double part, and cried
   And heard another's voice cry: 'What! are *you* here?'
Although we were not. I was still the same,
   Knowing myself yet being someone other—
   And he a face still forming; yet the words sufficed
To compel the recognition they preceded.
   And so, compliant to the common wind,
   Too strange to each other for misunderstanding,
In concord at this intersection time
   Of meeting nowhere, no before and after,
   We trod the pavement in a dead patrol.
I said: 'The wonder that I feel is easy,
   Yet ease is cause of wonder. Therefore speak:
   I may not comprehend, may not remember.'
And he: 'I am not eager to rehearse
   My thought and theory which you have forgotten.
   These things have served their purpose: let them be.
So with your own, and pray they be forgiven
   By others, as I pray you to forgive
   Both bad and good. Last season's fruit is eaten

And the fullfed beast shall kick the empty pail.
　　For last year's words belong to last year's language
　　And next year's words await another voice.
But, as the passage now presents no hindrance
　　To the spirit unappeased and peregrine
　　Between two worlds become much like each other,
So I find words I never thought to speak
　　In streets I never thought I should revisit
　　When I left my body on a distant shore.
Since our concern was speech, and speech impelled us
　　To purify the dialect of the tribe
　　And urge the mind to aftersight and foresight,
Let me disclose the gifts reserved for age
　　To set a crown upon your lifetime's effort.
　　First, the cold friction of expiring sense
Without enchantment, offering no promise
　　But bitter tastelessness of shadow fruit
　　As body and soul begin to fall asunder.
Second, the conscious impotence of rage
　　At human folly, and the laceration
　　Of laughter at what ceases to amuse.
And last, the rending pain of re-enactment
　　Of all that you have done, and been; the shame
　　Of motives late revealed, and the awareness

Of things ill done and done to others' harm
  Which once you took for exercise of virtue.
  Then fools' approval stings, and honour stains.
From wrong to wrong the exasperated spirit
  Proceeds, unless restored by that refining fire
  Where you must move in measure, like a dancer.'
The day was breaking. In the disfigured street
  He left me, with a kind of valediction,
  And faded on the blowing of the horn.

III

There are three conditions which often look alike
Yet differ completely, flourish in the same hedgerow:
Attachment to self and to things and to persons, detachment
From self and from things and from persons; and, growing
        between them, indifference
Which resembles the others as death resembles life,
Being between two lives—unflowering, between
The live and the dead nettle. This is the use of memory:
For liberation—not less of love but expanding
Of love beyond desire, and so liberation
From the future as well as the past. Thus, love of a country
Begins as attachment to our own field of action

And comes to find that action of little importance
Though never indifferent. History may be servitude,
History may be freedom. See, now they vanish,
The faces and places, with the self which, as it could, loved them,
To become renewed, transfigured, in another pattern.

Sin is Behovely, but
All shall be well, and
All manner of thing shall be well.
If I think, again, of this place,
And of people, not wholly commendable,
Of no immediate kin or kindness,
But some of peculiar genius,
All touched by a common genius,
United in the strife which divided them;
If I think of a king at nightfall,
Of three men, and more, on the scaffold
And a few who died forgotten
In other places, here and abroad,
And of one who died blind and quiet
Why should we celebrate
These dead men more than the dying?
It is not to ring the bell backward
Nor is it an incantation
To summon the spectre of a Rose.

We cannot revive old factions
We cannot restore old policies
Or follow an antique drum.
These men, and those who opposed them
And those whom they opposed
Accept the constitution of silence
And are folded in a single party.
Whatever we inherit from the fortunate
We have taken from the defeated
What they had to leave us—a symbol:
A symbol perfected in death.
And all shall be well and
All manner of thing shall be well
By the purification of the motive
In the ground of our beseeching.

IV

The dove descending breaks the air
With flame of incandescent terror
Of which the tongues declare
The one discharge from sin and error.
The only hope, or else despair
    Lies in the choice of pyre or pyre—
    To be redeemed from fire by fire.

Who then devised the torment? Love.
Love is the unfamiliar Name
Behind the hands that wove
The intolerable shirt of flame
Which human power cannot remove.
We only live, only suspire
Consumed by either fire or fire.

V

What we call the beginning is often the end
And to make an end is to make a beginning.
The end is where we start from. And every phrase
And sentence that is right (where every word is at home,
Taking its place to support the others,
The word neither diffident nor ostentatious,
An easy commerce of the old and the new,
The common word exact without vulgarity,
The formal word precise but not pedantic,
The complete consort dancing together)
Every phrase and every sentence is an end and a beginning,
Every poem an epitaph. And any action
Is a step to the block, to the fire, down the sea's throat
Or to an illegible stone: and that is where we start.

We die with the dying:
See, they depart, and we go with them.
We are born with the dead:
See, they return, and bring us with them.
The moment of the rose and the moment of the yew-tree
Are of equal duration. A people without history
Is not redeemed from time, for history is a pattern
Of timeless moments. So, while the light fails
On a winter's afternoon, in a secluded chapel
History is now and England.

With the drawing of this Love and the voice of this Calling
We shall not cease from exploration
And the end of all our exploring
Will be to arrive where we started
And know the place for the first time.
Through the unknown, remembered gate
When the last of earth left to discover
Is that which was the beginning;
At the source of the longest river
The voice of the hidden waterfall
And the children in the apple-tree
Not known, because not looked for
But heard, half-heard, in the stillness

Between two waves of the sea.
Quick now, here, now, always—
A condition of complete simplicity
(Costing not less than everything)
And all shall be well and
All manner of thing shall be well
When the tongues of flame are in-folded
Into the crowned knot of fire
And the fire and the rose are one.

T. S. Eliot was born on September 26, 1888, in St. Louis, Missouri. From his first book, Prufrock and Other Observations *(1917), to* The Waste Land *(1922), to* Four Quartets *(1943), Eliot was a leader of the modernist movement in poetry and one of the most influential poets and critics of the twentieth century. He was awarded the Nobel Prize in 1948. He died on January 4, 1965, in London.*

RANDALL JARRELL

THE ORIENT EXPRESS

One looks from the train
Almost as one looked as a child. In the sunlight
What I see still seems to me plain,
I am safe; but at evening
As the lands darken, a questioning
Precariousness comes over everything.

Once after a day of rain
I lay longing to be cold; and after a while
I was cold again, and hunched shivering
Under the quilt's many colors, gray
With the dull ending of the winter day.
Outside me there were a few shapes
Of chairs and tables, things from a primer;
Outside the window
There were the chairs and tables of the world. . . .
I saw that the world
That had seemed to me the plain
Gray mask of all that was strange
Behind it—of all that *was*—was all.

But it is beyond belief.
One thinks, "Behind everything
An unforced joy, an unwilling
Sadness (a willing sadness, a forced joy)
Moves changelessly"; one looks from the train
And there is something, the same thing
Behind everything: all these little villages,
A passing woman, a field of grain,
The man who says good-bye to his wife—

A path through a wood full of lives, and the train
Passing, after all unchangeable
And not now ever to stop, like a heart—

It is like any other work of art.
It is and never can be changed.
Behind everything there is always
The unknown unwanted life.

Randall Jarrell was born on May 6, 1914, in Nashville, Tennessee. An important literary critic as well as a poet, his essays are collected in Poetry and the Age *(1953), among others. His second-to-last book of poems,* The Woman at the Washington Zoo, *won the National Book Award in 1961. He died on October 14, 1965, in Chapel Hill, North Carolina.*

JOHN BERRYMAN

THERE SAT DOWN, ONCE

There sat down, once, a thing on Henry's heart
só heavy, if he had a hundred years
& more, & weeping, sleepless, in all them time
Henry could not make good.
Starts again always in Henry's ears
the little cough somewhere, an odour, a chime.

And there is another thing he has in mind
like a grave Sienese face a thousand years
would fail to blur the still profiled reproach of. Ghastly,
with open eyes, he attends, blind.
All the bells say: too late. This is not for tears;
thinking.

But never did Henry, as he thought he did,
end anyone and hacks her body up
and hide the pieces, where they may be found.
He knows: he went over everyone, & nobody's missing.
Often he reckons, in the dawn, them up.
Nobody is ever missing.

John Berryman was born on October 25, 1914, in McAlester, Oklahoma. His important books of verse include Homage to Mistress Bradstreet *(1956),* 77 Dream Songs *(1964), and* His Toy, His Dream, His Rest *(1968). His memoir,* Recovery, *was published posthumously in 1973. He committed suicide on January 7, 1972, in Minneapolis.*

W. H. AUDEN

SECRETS

That we are always glad
When the Ugly Princess, parting the bushes
To find out why the woodcutter's children are happy,
Disturbs a hornets' nest, that we feel no pity
When the informer is trapped by the gang in a steam-room,
That we howl with joy
When the short-sighted Professor of Icelandic

Pronounces the Greek inscription
A Runic riddle which he then translates:

Denouncing by proxy our commonest fault as our worst;
That, waiting in his room for a friend,
We start so soon to turn over his letters,
That with such assurance we repeat as our own
Another's story, that, dear me, how often
We kiss in order to tell,
Defines precisely what we mean by love:—
To share a secret.

The joke, which we seldom see, is on us;
For only true hearts know how little it matters
What the secret is they keep:
An old, a new, a blue, a borrowed something,
Anything will do for children
Made in God's image and therefore
Not like the others, not like our dear dumb friends
Who, poor things, have nothing to hide,
Not, thank God, like our Father either
From whom no secrets are hid.

W. H. Auden was born on February 21, 1907, in York, England. A prolific poet, playwright, librettist, critic, editor, and translator, Auden was a hero of the Left during the Great Depression, went to Spain in 1937 during the civil war, and immigrated to America in 1939. The Age of Anxiety won the Pulitzer Prize in 1948 and The Shield of Achilles won the National Book Award in 1956. Auden died on September 29, 1973, in Vienna.

MARIANNE MOORE

A GRAVE

Man looking into the sea,
taking the view from those who have as much right to it as
                                        you have to it yourself,
it is human nature to stand in the middle of a thing,
but you cannot stand in the middle of this;
the sea has nothing to give but a well excavated grave.
The firs stand in a procession, each with an emerald turkey-foot at the top,
reserved as their contours, saying nothing;

repression, however, is not the most obvious characteristic of the sea;
the sea is a collector, quick to return a rapacious look.
There are others besides you who have worn that look—
whose expression is no longer a protest; the fish no longer investigate them
for their bones have not lasted:
men lower nets, unconscious of the fact that they are desecrating a grave,
and row quickly away—the blades of the oars
moving together like the feet of water-spiders as if there were

                                        no such thing as death.
The wrinkles progress among themselves in a phalanx—

                           beautiful under networks of foam,
and fade breathlessly while the sea rustles in and out of the seaweed;
the birds swim through the air at top speed, emitting cat-calls as heretofore—
the tortoise-shell scourges about the feet of the cliffs, in motion

                                     beneath them;
and the ocean, under the pulsation of lighthouses and noise of bell-buoys,
advances as usual, looking as if it were not that ocean in which

                              dropped things are bound to sink—
in which if they turn and twist, it is neither with volition nor consciousness.

Marianne Moore was born on November 15, 1887, in St. Louis, Missouri. Her first two volumes, Poems *(1921) and* Observations *(1924), already exhibited her acute vision and analysis of her subjects. She won both the Pulitzer Prize and the Bollingen Prize for her* Collected Poems, *which was published in 1951. Moore died on February 5, 1972, in New York City.*

EZRA POUND

from HOMAGE TO SEXTUS PROPERTIUS

Orfeo   *"Quia pauper amavi."*

I

Shades of Callimachus, Coan ghosts of Philetas
It is in your grove I would walk,
I who come first from the clear font
Bringing the Grecian orgies into Italy,
                    and the dance into Italy.

Who hath taught you so subtle a measure,
                    in what hall have you heard it;
What foot beat out your time-bar,
                    what water has mellowed your whistles?

Out-weariers of Apollo will, as we know, continue their Martian generalities,
        We have kept our erasers in order.
A new-fangled chariot follows the flower-hung horses;
A young Muse with young loves clustered about her
                    ascends with me into the æther, . . .
And there is no high-road to the Muses.

Annalists will continue to record Roman reputations,
Celebrities from the Trans-Caucasus will belaud Roman celebrities
And expound the distentions of Empire,
But for something to read in normal circumstances?
For a few pages brought down from the forked hill unsullied?
I ask a wreath which will not crush my head.
                    And there is no hurry about it;
I shall have, doubtless, a boom after my funeral,
Seeing that long standing increases all things
                        regardless of quality.

And who would have known the towers
                    pulled down by a deal-wood horse;
Or of Achilles withstaying waters by Simois

Or of Hector spattering wheel-rims,
Or of Polydmantus, by Scamander, or Helenus and Deiphoibos?
Their door-yards would scarcely know them, or Paris.
Small talk O Ilion, and O Troad
                                twice taken by Oetian gods,
If Homer had not stated your case!

And I also among the later nephews of this city
                                shall have my dog's day,
With no stone upon my contemptible sepulchre;
My vote coming from the temple of Phoebus in Lycia, at Patara,
And in the meantime my songs will travel,
And the devirginated young ladies will enjoy them
                        when they have got over the strangeness,
For Orpheus tamed the wild beasts—
                                and held up the Threician river;
And Cithaeron shook up the rocks by Thebes
            and danced them into a bulwark at his pleasure,
And you, O Polyphemus? Did harsh Galatea almost
Turn to your dripping horses, because of a tune, under Aetna?
We must look into the matter.
Bacchus and Apollo in favour of it,
There will be a crowd of young women doing homage to my palaver,
Though my house is not propped up by Taenarian columns from Laconia
    (associated with Neptune and Cerberus),
Though it is not stretched upon gilded beams;

My orchards do not lie level and wide
                    as the forests of Phaecia,
                    the luxurious and Ionian,.
Nor are my caverns stuffed stiff with a Marcian vintage,
My cellar does not date from Numa Pompilius,
Nor bristle with wine jars,
Nor is it equipped with a frigidaire patent;
Yet the companions of the Muses
                    will keep their collective nose in my books,
And weary with historical data, they will turn to my dance tune.

Happy who are mentioned in my pamphlets,
            the songs shall be a fine tomb-stone over their beauty.
                    But against this?
Neither expensive pyramids scraping the stars in their route,
Nor houses modelled upon that of Jove in East Elis,
Nor the monumental effigies of Mausolus,
                    are a complete elucidation of death.

Flame burns, rain sinks into the cracks
And they all go to rack ruin beneath the thud of the years.
Stands genius a deathless adornment,
            a name not to be worn out with the years.

Ezra Pound was born on October 30, 1885, in Hailey, Idaho. His poetry includes Hugh Selwyn Mauberley *and* The Cantos. *Pound was arrested by the Allies at the end of World War II and held until 1958 for pro-Fascist radio broadcasts he made in Italy during the war. He died in Venice on November 1, 1972.*

DAVID JONES

THE TUTELAR OF THE PLACE

She that loves place, time, demarcation, hearth, kin, enclosure,
site, differentiated cult, though she is but one mother of us all:
one earth brings us all forth, one womb receives us all, yet to each
she is other, named of some name other. . .

                           . . . other sons, beyond
hill, over strath, or never so neighbouring by nigh field or near

crannog up stream. What co-tidal line can plot if nigrin or flax-head marching their wattles be cognate or german of common totem?

Tellus of the myriad names answers to but one name: From this tump she answers Jac o'the Tump only if he call Great-Jill-of-the-tump-that-bare-me, not if he cry by some new fangle moder of far gentes over the flud, fer-goddes name from anaphora of far folk wont woo her; she's a rare one for locality. Or, gently she bends her head from far-height when tongue-strings chime the name she whispered on known-site, as between sister and brother at the time of beginnings... when the wrapped bands are cast and the worst mewling is over, after the weaning and before the august initiations, in the years of becoming.
When she and he 'twixt door-stone and fire-stane prefigure and puppet on narrow floor-stone and world-masque on wide world-floor.
When she attentively changes her doll-shift, lets pretend with solemnity as rocking the womb-gift.
When he chivvies house-pet with his toy *hasta*, makes believe the cat o'the wold falls to the pitiless bronze.
                    Man-travail and woman-war here we see enacted are.
            When she and he beside the settle, he and she between the trestle-struts, mime the bitter dance to come

Cheek by chin at the childer-crock where the quick tears drop
and the quick laughter dries the tears, within the rim of the shared
curd-cup each fore-reads the world-storm.
Till the spoil-sport gammers sigh:
                                        Now come on now little
children, come on now it's past the hour. Sun's to roost, brood's
in pent, dusk-star tops mound, lupa sniffs the lode-damps for
stragglers late to byre.
Come now it's time to come now for tarry awhile and slow
                        cot's best for yearlings
                        crib's best for babes
here's a rush to light you to bed
here's a fleece to cover your head
against the world-storm
                brother by sister
under one *brethyn*
kith of the kin warmed at the one hearth-flame
(of the seed of far-gaffer? fair gammer's wer-gifts?)
cribbed in the garth that the garth-Jill wards.

Though she inclines with attention from far fair-height outside
all boundaries, beyond the known and kindly nomenclatures,
where all names are one name, where all stones of demarcation
dance and interchange, troia the skipping mountains, nod
recognitions.

As when on known-site ritual frolics keep bucolic interval at
eves and divisions when they mark the inflexions of the year
and conjugate with trope and turn the season's syntax, with
beating feet, with wands and pentagons to spell out the
Trisagion.

Who laud and magnify with made, mutable and beggarly
elements the unmade immutable begettings and precessions of fair-
height, with halting sequences and unresolved rhythms, search-
ingly, with what's to hand, under the inconstant lights that hover
world-flats, that bright by fit and start of the tangle of world-wood,
rifting the dark drifts for the wanderers that wind the world-
meander, who seek hidden grammar to give back anathema its
first benignity.
Gathering all things in, twining each bruised stem to the swaying
trellis of the dance, the dance about the sawn lode-stake on the
hill where the hidden stillness is at the core of struggle, the dance
around the green lode-tree on far fair-height where the secret
guerdons hang and the bright prizes nod, where sits the queen
im Rosenhage eating the honey-cake, where the king sits, counting-
out his man-geld, rhyming the audits of all the world-holdings.

Where the marauder leaps the wall and the wall dances to the
marauder's leaping, where the plunging wolf-spear and the wolf's
pierced diaphragm sing the same song . . .

Yet, when she stoops to hear you children cry
            from the scattered and single habitations
or from the nucleated holdings
                        from tower'd *castra*
                        paved *civitas*
                        treble-ramped *caer*
                        or wattled *tref*
                                    stockaded *gorod* or
                                    trenched *burh*
from which ever child-crib within whatever enclosure
demarked by a dynast or staked by consent
wherever in which of the wide world-ridings
                        you must not call her but by that name
which accords to the morphology of that place.
Now pray now little children for us all now, pray our gammer's
prayer according to our *disciplina* given to us
within our labyrinth on our dark mountain.
                        Say now little children:
Sweet Jill of our hill hear us
bring slow bones safe at the lode-ford
keep lupa's bite without our wattles
make her bark keep children good
save us all from dux of far folk

save us from the men who plan.

Now sleep on, little children, sleep on now, while I tell out the greater suffrages, not yet for young heads to understand:

Queen of the differentiated sites, administratrix of the demarcations, let our cry come unto you.

              In all times of imperium save us when the *mercatores* come save us

        from the guile of the *negotiatores* save us from the *missi*, from the agents

           who think no shame
by inquest to audit what is shameful to tell

                 deliver us.
When they check their capitularies in their curias

            confuse their reckonings.
When they narrowly assess the *trefydd*

           by hide and rod

           by *pentan* and pent
by impost and fee on beast-head

           and roof-tree
and number the souls of men

             notch their tallies false
disorder what they have collated.

When they proscribe the diverse uses and impose the
rootless uniformities, pray for us.
                              When they sit in *Consilium*
to liquidate the holy diversities
                              mother of particular perfections
                              queen of otherness
                              mistress of asymmetry
patroness of things counter, parti, pied, several
protectress of things known and handled
help of things familiar and small
                              wardress of the secret crevices
                              of things wrapped and hidden
mediatrix of all the deposits
                              margravine of the troia
empress of the labyrinth
                              receive our prayers.
When they escheat to the Ram
                              in the Ram's curia
the seisin where the naiad sings
                              above where the forked rod bends
or where the dark outcrop
                              tells on the hidden seam
pray for the green valley.
When they come with writs of oyer and terminer
                              to hear the false and
                              determine the evil

according to the advices of the Ram's magnates who serve the
Ram's wife, who write in the Ram's book of Death.
In the bland megalopolitan light
      where no shadow is by day or by night
be our shadow.
Remember the mound-kin, the kith of the *tarren* gone from this
mountain because of the exorbitance of the Ram ... remember
them in the rectangular tenements, in the houses of the engines
that fabricate the ingenuities of the Ram ... Mother of Flowers
save them then where no flower blows.
                      Though they shall not come again
because of the requirements of the Ram with respect to the world
plan, remember them where the dead forms multiply, where no
stamen leans, where the carried pollen falls to the adamant surfaces,
where is no crevice.
In all times of *Gleichschaltung*, in the days of the central economies,
set up the hedges of illusion round some remnant of us, twine the
wattles of mist, white-web a Gwydion-hedge
      like a fog on the *bryniau*
      against the commissioners
and assessors bearing the writs of the Ram to square the world-
floor and number the tribes and write down the secret things and
take away the diversities by which we are, by which we call on
your name, sweet Jill of the demarcations

                    arc of differences
                       tower of individuation
                       queen of the minivers
laughing in the mantle of variety
belle of the mound
                        for Jac o' the mound
our belle and donnabelle
                            on all the world-mountain.
In the December of our culture ward somewhere the secret seed,
under the mountain, under and between, between the grids of
the Ram's survey when he squares the world-circle.
Sweet Mair devise a mazy-guard
in and out and round about
double-dance defences
countermure and echelon meanders round
the holy mound
                    fence within the fence
pile the dun ash for the bright seed
                    (within the curtained wood the canister
within the canister the budding rod)
troia in depth the shifting wattles of illusion for the ancilia for the
palladia for the kept memorials, because of the commissioners
of the Ram and the Ram's decree concerning the utility of the
hidden things.

When the technicians manipulate the dead limbs of our culture
as though it yet had life, have mercy on us. Open unto us, let us
enter a second time within your stola-folds in those days—
ventricle and refuge both, *hendref* for world-winter, asylum from
world-storm. Womb of the Lamb the spoiler of the Ram.

c. 1960 incorporating passages written earlier

Vernon Watkins provided a glossary of certain Welsh words in this poem:

brethyn	cloth	*tarren*	tump, knoll
bryniau	hills	*tref*	hamlet
caer	fort, castle, city	*trefydd*	hamlets
hendref	ancestral dwelling, winter quarters	*troia*	meander, from *troi*, to turn, and Troea, Troy.
pentam	hob, fire-stone		

David Jones was born on November 1, 1895, in Brockley, England. Primarily a painter, Jones also wrote poetry. His most important book is In Parenthesis *(1937), a long seven-part poem drawn from his experiences as an infantry soldier in World War I. Jones also worked as an engraver and illustrator. He died on October 28, 1974, in Harrow, England.*

ROBERT LOWELL

DOLPHIN

My Dolphin, you only guide me by surprise,
a captive as Racine, the man of craft,
drawn through his maze of iron composition
by the incomparable wandering voice of Phèdre.
When I was troubled in mind, you made for my body
caught in its hangman's-knot of sinking lines,
the glassy bowing and scraping of my will. . . .

I have sat and listened to too many
words of the collaborating muse,
and plotted perhaps too freely with my life,
not avoiding injury to others,
not avoiding injury to myself—
to ask compassion . . . this book, half fiction,
an eelnet made by man for the eel fighting—

my eyes have seen what my hand did.

Robert Lowell was born on March 1, 1917, in Boston. Lowell's reputation as a poet was established by his first commercially printed book, Lord Weary's Castle, *which won the Pulitzer Prize in 1947. His other books include the influential* Life Studies *(1959), which won the National Book Award,* Notebook 1967–68 *(1969), and* The Dolphin *(1973), for which he won his second Pulitzer Prize. He died on September 12, 1977, in New York City.*

ELIZABETH BISHOP

THE IMAGINARY ICEBERG

We'd rather have the iceberg than the ship,
although it meant the end of travel.
Although it stood stock-still like cloudy rock
and all the sea were moving marble.
We'd rather have the iceberg than the ship;
we'd rather own this breathing plain of snow

though the ship's sails were laid upon the sea
as the snow lies undissolved upon the water.
O solemn, floating field,
are you aware an iceberg takes repose
with you, and when it wakes may pasture on your snows?

This is a scene a sailor'd give his eyes for.
The ship's ignored. The iceberg rises
and sinks again; its glassy pinnacles
correct elliptics in the sky.
This is a scene where he who treads the boards
is artlessly rhetorical. The curtain
is light enough to rise on finest ropes
that airy twists of snow provide.
The wits of these white peaks
spar with the sun. Its weight the iceberg dares
upon a shifting stage and stands and stares.

This iceberg cuts its facets from within.
Like jewelry from a grave
it saves itself perpetually and adorns
only itself, perhaps the snows
which so surprise us lying on the sea.

Good-bye, we say, good-bye, the ship steers off
where waves give in to one another's waves
and clouds run in a warmer sky.
Icebergs behoove the soul
(both being self-made from elements least visible)
to see them so: fleshed, fair, erected indivisible.

Elizabeth Bishop was born on February 8, 1911, in Worcester, Massachusetts. Raised in Nova Scotia and educated in the United States, Bishop lived in Petrópolis, near Rio de Janeiro, Brazil, for most of the 1950s and 1960s. Her books include North and South, *which won the Pulitzer Prize in 1956,* Questions of Travel, *and* Geography III. The Complete Poems, *published in 1969, won the National Book Award. She died in Boston on October 6, 1979.*

JAMES WRIGHT

IN RESPONSE TO A RUMOR THAT THE OLDEST WHOREHOUSE IN WHEELING, WEST VIRGINIA, HAS BEEN CONDEMNED

I will grieve alone,
As I strolled alone, years ago, down along
The Ohio shore.
I hid in the hobo jungle weeds
Upstream from the sewer main,
Pondering, gazing.

I saw, down river,
At Twenty-third and Water Streets
By the vinegar works,
The doors open in early evening.
Swinging their purses, the women
Poured down the long street to the river
And into the river.

I do not know how it was
They could drown every evening.
What time near dawn did they climb up the other shore,
Drying their wings?

For the river at Wheeling, West Virginia,
Has only two shores:
The one in hell, the other
In Bridgeport, Ohio.

And nobody would commit suicide, only
To find beyond death
Bridgeport, Ohio.

James Wright was born on December 13, 1927, in Martin's Ferry, Ohio. His books include The Branch Will Not Break *(1963),* Collected Poems *(1971), for which he won the Pulitzer Prize,* This Journey *(1982), and his complete poems,* Above the River, *published in 1990. He died on March 25, 1980, in New York City.*

HOWARD MOSS

THE PRUNED TREE

As a torn paper might seal up its side,
Or a streak of water stitch itself to silk
And disappear, my wound has been my healing,
And I am made more beautiful by losses.
See the flat water in the distance nodding
Approval, the light that fell in love with statues,
Seeing me alive, turn its motion toward me.
Shorn, I rejoice in what was taken from me.

What can the moonlight do with my new shape
But trace and retrace its miracle of order?
I stand, waiting for the strange reaction
Of insects who knew me in my larger self,
Unkempt, in a naturalness I did not love.
Even the dog's voice rings with a new echo,
And all the little leaves I shed are singing,
Singing to the moon of shapely newness.

Somewhere what I lost I hope is springing
To life again. The roofs, astonished by me,
Are taking new bearings in the night, the owl
Is crying for a further wisdom, the lilac
Putting forth its strongest scent to find me.
Butterflies, the sailboat's grooves, are winging
Out of the water to wash me, wash me.
Now, I am stirring like a seed in China.

Howard Moss was born on January 22, 1922, in New York City. Moss was the author of twelve books of poetry, including his Selected Poems, *which won the National Book Award in 1972. Moss was also an accomplished playwright and the poetry editor of* The New Yorker *for almost forty years. He died in New York City on September 16, 1987.*

ROBERT GRAVES

TO JUAN AT THE WINTER SOLSTICE

There is one story and one story only
That will prove worth your telling,
Whether as learned bard or gifted child;
To it all lines or lesser gauds belong
That startle with their shining
Such common stories as they stray into.

Is it of trees you tell, their months and virtues,
Or strange beasts that beset you,
Of birds that croak at you the Triple will?
Or of the Zodiac and how slow it turns
Below the Boreal Crown,
Prison of all true kings that ever reigned?

Water to water, ark again to ark,
From woman back to woman:
So each new victim treads unfalteringly
The never altered circuit of his fate,
Bringing twelve peers as witness
Both to his starry rise and starry fall.

Or is it of the Virgin's silver beauty,
All fish below the thighs?
She in her left hand bears a leafy quince;
When with her right she crooks a finger, smiling,
How may the King hold back?
Royally then he barters life for love.

Or of the undying snake from chaos hatched,
Whose coils contain the ocean,
Into whose chops with naked sword he springs,

Then in black water, tangled by the reeds,
Battles three days and nights,
To be spewed up beside her scalloped shore?

Much snow is falling, winds roar hollowly,
The owl hoots from the elder,
Fear in your heart cries to the loving-cup:
Sorrow to sorrow as the sparks fly upward.
The log groans and confesses:
There is one story and one story only.

Dwell on her graciousness, dwell on her smiling,
Do not forget what flowers
The great boar trampled down in ivy time.
Her brow was creamy as the crested wave,
Her sea-blue eyes were wild
But nothing promised that is not performed.

Robert Graves was born on July 24, 1895, in London. Graves's Collected Poems, *first published in 1948, was revised a fourth time in 1975. He was also author of a memoir about World War I,* Good-Bye to All That *(1929), the novel* I, Claudius, *and the study* The White Goddess. *He died on December 7, 1985, in Deyá, on the island of Majorca, Spain.*

HOWARD NEMEROV

DANDELIONS

These golden heads, these common suns
Only less multitudinous
Than grass itself that gluts
The market of the world with green,
They shine as lovely as they're mean,
Fine as the daughters of the poor
Who go proudly in spangles of brass;
Light-headed, then headless, stalked for a salad.

Inside a week they will be seen
Stricken and old, ghosts in the field
To be picked up at the lightest breath,
With brazen tops all shrunken in
And swollen green gone withered white.
You'll say it's nature's price for beauty
That goes cheap; that being light
Is justly what makes girls grow heavy;
And that the wind, bearing their death,
Whispers the second kingdom come.
—You'll say, the fool of piety,
By resignations hanging on
Until, still justified, you drop.
But surely the thing is sorrowful,
At evening, when the light goes out
Slowly, to see those ruined spinsters,
All down the field their ghostly hair,
Dry sinners waiting in the valley
For the last word and the next life
And the liberation from the lion's mouth.

Howard Nemerov was born on March 1, 1920, in New York City. Nemerov served as a pilot from 1941 until 1945 in World War II and afterward taught English at colleges in America. He was poet laureate of the United States from 1988 until 1990. The Collected Poems of Howard Nemerov, *published in 1977, won both the Pulitzer Prize and the National Book Award. Nemerov died on July 5, 1991, in University City, Missouri.*

WILLIAM STAFFORD

AT THE BOMB TESTING SITE

At noon in the desert a panting lizard
waited for history, its elbows tense,
watching the curve of a particular road
as if something might happen.

It was looking at something farther off
than people could see, an important scene

acted in stone for little selves
at the flute end of consequences.

There was just a continent without much on it
under a sky that never cared less.
Ready for a change, the elbows waited.
The hands gripped hard on the desert.

William Stafford was born on January 17, 1914, in Hutchinson, Kansas. His books include Stories That Could Be True *(1977),* Smoke's Way *(1983), and* My Name Is William Tell *(1992). His memoir* Down in My Heart *(1947) is about his experiences as a conscientious objector in World War II. He served as consultant in poetry to the Library of Congress from 1970 until 1971. Stafford died on August 28, 1993, in Lake Oswego, Oregon.*

JAMES MERRILL

AN UPWARD LOOK

O heart green acre   sown with salt
by the departing   occupier

lay down your gallant   spears of wheat
Salt of the earth   each stellar pinch

flung in blind   defiance backwards
now takes its toll   Up from his quieted

quarry the lover   colder and wiser
hauling himself   finds the world turning

toys triumphs   toxins into
this vast facility   the living come
dearest to die in   How did it happen

In bright alternation   minutely mirrored
within the thinking   of each and every

mortal creature   halves of a clue
approach the earthlights   Morning star

evening star   salt of the sky
First the grave   dissolving into dawn

then the crucial   recrystallizing
from inmost depths   of clear dark blue

James Merrill was born on March 3, 1926, in New York City. His epic poem trilogy—Divine Comedies *(1976),* Mirabell: Books of Number *(1978), for which he won his second National Book Award, and* Scripts for the Pageant *(1980)—was collected in the volume* The Changing Light at Sandover *in 1982. His memoir,* A Different Person, *was published in 1993 and his last book of poems,* A Scattering of Salts, *was published posthumously in 1995. Merrill died on February 6, 1995, in Tucson.*